CLARITY IS POWER

Q&A

"Clarity is Power" book series, is a collection of wisdom from thought-provoking Q and A with renowned Mahatria. His unique gift of answering questions spontaneously is captured in this book, offering life-changing insights.

The "Clarity is Power" series comprises 11 illuminating volumes, each addressing essential aspects of life:

1. Attitudes
2. Self-Discipline
3. Emotional Development
4. Relationships
5. Marriage
6. Parenting
7. Student Life
8. Career Growth
9. Leadership and Entrepreneurship
10. Spirituality
11. Faith

Mahatria Spiritualist | Thought leader | Diviner of infinitheism

For nearly three decades, Mahatria has empowered millions worldwide to achieve holistic abundance. His profound wisdom uplifts people in health, wealth, love, bliss, and spirituality.

infinitheism, the path divined by Mahatria, inspires breakthroughs for anyone who ardently desires abundance by transforming the human spirit to have faith in its infinite potential.

First published in India

MANJUL

Manjul Publishing House

• 2nd Floor, Usha Preet Complex,
42 Malviya Nagar, Bhopal 462 003 - India
• C-16, Sector 3, Noida, Uttar Pradesh 201301 – India
Website: www.manjulindia.com

Distribution Centres:
Ahmedabad, Bengaluru, Bhopal, Kolkata, Chennai,
Hyderabad, Mumbai, New Delhi, Pune

In association with:

infinitheism

3, 3rd Cross Road, R A Puram,
Chennai, Tamil Nadu, India
www.infinitheism.com

STUDENT LIFE (CLARITY IS POWER)

by

mahatria Rā

This edition first published in 2016
Third impression 2024

ISBN 978-93-5543-429-6

Printed and bound in India by Thomson Press (India) Ltd.

CLARITY IS POWER

Q&A

STUDENT LIFE

mahātria

CONTENTS

CONTENTS

I am in twelfth. I feel my mother loves my younger sister more than she loves me. This is affecting my studies a lot. Please help me.

The best solution to your problem is to love your younger sister even more than your mother loves her. Let us say you like the actor Rajinikanth a lot and your mother too loves him a lot - will you have a problem? In fact, liking Rajinikanth will amount to liking you. Enjoy the toy your mother is enjoying, and now you will enjoy the toy, as well as your mother.

What you go through is common even amongst adults. More or less attention is perceived as more or less love. Attention is equated to love. The fact is that your younger sister is enjoying more attention from your mother but that doesn't imply she is being loved more. You will understand this when you grow up.

Stop seeing your younger sister as your rival. See her as yours; not as your mother's. Become absolutely demonstrative and expressive of your love for her. As a result, how your mother relates to your little sister will become absolutely inconsequential to you. ●

2

My desire is to excel in all subjects and become the school topper. But I feel I can't. How to overcome this feeling and excel?

In the movie 'Pursuit Of Happyness', the father tells the son: “Don't ever let someone tell you, you can't do something. Not even me. You got a dream, you got to protect it. People can't do something themselves, they want to tell you, you can't do it. You want something; go get it. Period.”

An ant told a human being, “People block my path, but I find an alternate path and keep marching. Whatever be the obstacles, however difficult the hurdles, I carry on with the belief, 'I Can'. Till I die, I try, I fight, I strive and I keep living with the belief, 'I Can'. I lose this sense of ‘I Can' only to death. If this is what I can do as an ant, hey man, how much is possible by you... if only you too believe, 'I Can'.”

The heart of a person told the person, “I began beating when you were in the womb of your mother and I will keep beating till you reach the tomb. Relentlessly I keep working with so much intensity and enthusiasm. And, I know 'I Can' till the end... after all, if not, that will be the end. If this is what I can do as just an organ of your body, hey man, as the master of this body, is it not possible for you to work with relentless intensity and enthusiasm in whatever you do... if only you too believe, 'I Can'.”

The hand of a person told the person, "I dirty myself to keep the other parts of the body clean. If anybody tries to hurt any part of the body, I volunteer to take the hurt unto myself, and protect the other parts of the body. I know 'I Can' and I will take responsibility for every part of the body I belong to. If this is what I can do as just a part in your body, hey man, is it not possible for you to assume responsibility for the welfare of all your near and dear ones... if only you too believe, 'I Can'."

The leg of a person told the person, "I take you wherever you want to go. I help you to reach whatever be the destination. I always believe, 'I Can'. If this is what I can do as just a part in your body, hey man, is it not possible for you to arrive at every goal you set for yourself, accomplish every ambition of yours, and fulfil every dream you have dreamt for yourself... if only you too believe, 'I Can'."

Bumblebee is an insect with disproportionately small wings compared to the size of its body. Scientists from aerodynamics have concluded that a bumblebee cannot fly for this very reason. Fortunately the bumblebee does not understand science or the scientists. So it keeps flying. You can be a bumblebee.

It doesn't matter whether others believe in you or not, you got to believe 'I Can', and if you do, you can become whatever you want to become. It does not matter, even if everybody believes in you and if you don't believe in yourself. Ironically, even if nobody believes in you and if you believe in yourself, it matters a lot. The language of life is 'I can.' You want something; go get it. Period.

> *Is it true that the power of 'words' play a major role in the shaping of a personality?*

My very life is a validation of the truth, "Your words create your world." John 1:1 says, "In the beginning was the Word, and the Word was with God, and the Word was God." If God represents 'Creation', then my life is an experiential validation to 'Word was God'.

Though I was average in academics and not all that good either at grammar or with spelling, I always had a flair for words. Words always caught my attention, and they still do. Even today, the mobile app that I use the most is 'WordWeb'. Even today, I feel energised when I get to tongue new words.

Sai Madhavan was my classmate during graduation from 1982 to 1985. He is a lexophile - a lover of words. Most of Sai's discussions used to be about English, grammar, words, and also about making it very big in the future.

Narayanan, another classmate of mine, who was also involved with shorthand practices, was always coming up with new words. They would talk about words like tête-à-tête or rendezvous, and once I learnt the meaning, my mind used to process it, "One day I should call somebody for a tête-à-tête." They would use a phrase like 'assert with aplomb', and my mind used to think, “Where can I use this?” So, during the early days in my career, the last sentence in all my job applications read, “Given an opportunity, I can assert with aplomb that I will more than live up to your expectations.” During those days, all my formal communication used to have a sentence starting with, “I am sanguine...” ever since I heard from Sai and Narayanan that 'sanguine' means 'cheerfully and confidently optimistic'.

I vividly remember, in 1984, a colleague of mine used the word 'magnanimous' to describe my first boss. The word sounded very good on my ears. When I returned home, I went straight for the dictionary. Once I understood the meaning, I developed a deep desire to grow up to be worthy of the word - 'magnanimous'.

Between 1992 and 1994, during my active association with Aporesh Acharya, who is considered as the Father of personality development training in India, what impacted me the most was the way Aporesh would say, “Top of the World.” I too started saying 'Top of the World' and eventually started feeling on 'Top of the World'. I owe the quality of my life to this magical phrase and its source - Aporesh, “Top of the World.”

Scriptures or Gurus didn't lure me into spirituality, but I was magnetised by the meaning and the depth of words like abundance, enthusiasm, blessing, faith, surrender, entrainment, devotion, flowing, presence, divine, theism, infinite, cosmos, grace, radiance, transcendence, epiphany, love, bliss, purity and gratitude. Even just saying these words kept purifying something within me. There was an introverted pull in these words. Eventually, the depth and the meaning of these words dissolved into the core of my being, resulting in me living out of this spiritual fragrance. By embracing the words of a higher tongue, you do embrace the life of a higher consciousness. By giving up the words of a lower tongue, you do transcend the life of animalistic consciousness.

My very life is testimony to the truth: Because your words create your world, in some ways, 'Word is God'. ●

I am not fluent in English. I did most of my education in Telugu. My friends laugh at my English. What books should I read to speak better English?

Spoken language cannot be developed through books. Only being in an environment where that language is being spoken will develop fluency in that language. Have you noticed that people who are very good at reading and writing in Sanskrit, are not necessarily able to speak in Sanskrit. Professors who can teach English cannot necessarily speak at length in English. And, not necessarily all good orators are good at reading or writing in that language.

Environment alone can condition spoken language. You can observe how environment affects even the accent with which a language is spoken. An Indian exposed to an American environment long enough, gets conditioned to that accent. A classic example of this is the homemaker. On account of career-based relocation to a location with a different local language, the man rarely picks up the local language because he continues to communicate in the language of comfort at his workplace. However, the homemaker has to deal with the domestic help, vendors, marketplace, etc., and all of those communicate only in the local language. She has no choice but to become one with that environment. As a result she becomes proficient in the local language in a couple of years. In the mean time, the man generally manages to learn a couple of bad words and just a few instructional phrases in the local language.

Children cannot even pick up their mother tongue if they do not get exposed to an environment in which the mother tongue is spoken. On the other hand, expose children to multiple environments a particular language environment at home, one at school, one in the locality they grow up in, another where they go for their coaching classes - and you will find they become proficient communicators in all the languages. The bottom line is, environment is everything for the development of a spoken language.

There is no disgrace in not being good at a foreign language - people are not even good at their mother tongue. Inadequacy in a language is just an inadequacy. There is no shame in it. Most people live their whole life bragging about a weakness of theirs. Escapism is the easiest option, but that's not what you are seeking. In fact, you should feel very proud that you want to develop yourself in an area of your weakness. You are willing to do anything to overcome this impediment.

Just hurl yourself into an environment of English speaking people. Don't mind the mistakes. Don't mind being laughed at. Don't care for the sarcastic remarks you are bound to hear. Your mission is 'fluency in English' and not impressing others. Just keep speaking in English. Only speaking in that language can develop your skills in that language.

> *I am a medical student. I have no fire. I have no interest in anything. I have no will. I am very irresponsible too. I don't push myself to do anything. My parents are unhappy with me and so am I. I tried so many things, but nothing works.*

Surely, you are a case study. Oh, I am just kidding. Without an underlying passion to be somebody in life you would not have written this question to me. The very fact you have asked this question only means there is a spark within you. Now, start from where you can start. Move the pebbles before you desire to move the mountains. A small change sustained long enough becomes a monumental change. Begin from where you can begin.

One of the laws of life is, "You do not get in life what you desire; you only get what you deserve." How to attain that deservingness? When desires are backed up with Consistent, Directed, Self-motivated, Intelligent, Effort (C.D.S.I.E.), they become deservingness.

Even effortlessness is achieved only through effort. Life is about 1% inspiration and 99% perspiration. A friend of mine once remarked, "If I am not as intelligent as others, I can't help it. It is God's mistake. If I am not emotionally stable, I will accept it. It is a parenting mistake. However, if I don't put in more effort than others, I will never be able to excuse myself because it'll be my mistake."

Effort without intelligence is labour. Effort with intelligence is competence. Improving your competence is a lifelong striving. Even the best can be bettered. Keep asking, "How else? What else? Where else? Can I improve?"

All great people never stopped learning. To the last day of their life, they kept learning. Never go to sleep unless you have answered to yourself, "What did I learn for the day?"

Schooling will stop but let learning never stop. Learning stimulates intelligence. Develop your competence continuously.

I know you are saying, "That's the problem. I don't have the motivation to put in that intelligent effort."

Self-motivation alone can be sustained motivation. The spark has to come from within. However, since you are saying you don't have that self-motivation, let's embrace external motivation. See, even I don't enjoy pushing myself in jogging. So I get on to the treadmill, which pushes me. Getting on to the treadmill is my responsibility. From there the treadmill takes over. Whenever I don't feel like accomplishing a task, I make public commitments. Now, there is all round pressure. Else, I will fall in everyone's eyes. Oh, I want to grow in my own eyes and in everyone's eyes. So I rise to the occasion. Till you become a self-starter use the power of public commitments to be your kick-starter.

“There is nothing so useless as doing efficiently that which should not be done at all,” says Peter Drucker. Self-motivated intelligent effort without a sense of direction will be a waste of effort, time and energy. What's the point in reaching the top of the ladder and then realising that the ladder is leaning against the wrong wall? Time and effort can never be managed in isolation. It is always in the context of what you want from life and where you want to reach in life. Activity without direction is change. Activity with direction is progress.

I have this doubt that may be you were forced into medicine. Your heart is seeking something else and circumstances have pushed you into medicine. For the sake of making your medical seat count pursue this as your direction. Realise that someone in the world has been deprived of this seat on which you are sitting, and pursue this as your direction. Become aware that this direction will enable you to one day save lives, and pursue this as your direction.

Consistency is the hallmark of greatness. You will not be remembered for what you do or did once in a way, but for what you do and did all the time. Doesn't matter whether the act is small or big, but engage yourself in disciplines that you will practice on a daily basis, and this consistency will light the fire, that you are so dearly seeking, into you.

If you do not know how to take care of yourself, find a good mentor and hand your life over to him. He will know what to do with you. Nothing like growing in the right hands! Nothing like growing in the hands of the right teacher! ●

When desires are backed up with
Consistent
Directed
Self-motivated
Intelligent
Effort
(C.D.S.I.E.),
they become deservingness.

mahātria

6

My mother says, "If you don't get good grades, even a beggar will not respect you." My father says, "Without personality, your marks mean nothing. Join the NCC." I don't know if I can do justice to both. What should I do?

Nothing should happen at the cost of something. The question is no more, "WHICH is the best of everything", but it is, "HOW to get the best of everything?". The question is, "How to get Most and more... in all the dimensions of your life that will make your life complete."

First understand that every human being has Multiple Intelligences. Your ability to understand, appreciate and perform music is one form of intelligence - Musical Intelligence. This is completely different from your ability to think in pictures. If you are capable of thinking in pictures, if you are creative, then that's Spatial Intelligence. The ability to use your body beyond the mere day-to-day functioning is Bodily Intelligence, which is needed for someone to succeed in sports. The ability to relate with other people is Interpersonal Intelligence. So on and so forth you have Multiple Intelligences.

People who go to top are people who develop Multiple Intelligences. A singer who also knows to communicate well is always a better singer than the one who knows only to sing. That's Shankar Mahadevan's edge, a great singer who is also a good communicator. A cricketer who is also good at relating with other people is certainly a better player. That's Mahendra Singh Dhoni's edge, a good cricketer who is great in relationships.

A student who knows four languages has an advantage over those who know only three languages. A student who knows three languages has an advantage over those who know only two languages. That's why Indian students always do well in America. Indian students have the edge of knowing more than one language.

You want to be able-minded, you want to be competent, you want to have an edge over the rest, and then you are left with no choice but to develop yourself in Multiple Intelligence. This is where the role of extra-curricular activities comes in, to develop your Multiple Intelligence. No point in being a mere bookworm. Holistic development is necessary.

Those who develop Multiple Intelligences are always spotted in a crowd. So this year, as you go back to your school, not only focus on your academic brilliance, but also focus on developing yourself in Multiple Intelligences. Participate in at least one extra-curricular activity - either in school or out of school, and develop your Multiple Intelligences.

One of the most important aspects of Multiple Intelligences is your academic intelligence. Education expands your mind. Education makes all the difference. So, you must focus on Education also.

You should aspire to become more educated, much more educated than your parents and this is the best gift you can gift your parents. Work hard, systematise, and take help from your parents and teachers.

You need to develop your personality through extra-curricular activities, and also study very well. Both should be done and it is possible.

7

I see my classmates copying during exams and passing out with good marks. Though I don't wish to, I am tempted to copy too as it seems a much easier way. What should I do?

I am sure you know my answer. The satisfaction you get out of cooking that one brinjal, which came out of your own labour, is far greater than a kilogram of stolen brinjals. The question isn't what is easy and what is not. The question is what is right and what is not. Every time you choose the right over the wrong, you build yourself into a person of substance, which will make all the difference to your future.

My dear little one, eventually it isn't the marks that will take you to the top. It will be your personality, and the character traits with which you have built your personality that will help to leave a mark. If you start looking for crooked ways, you will eventually become a crook. There are no easy ways to the top. There are no shortcuts in life.

Winning a lottery may give you some immediate funds, but they don't keep you rich. The ways of your classmates may help them up to a point in life, but it will eventually forsake them. Work hard, my child. Put in the effort. If you do not get as much marks as the best in your class, that's okay. But if your effort is not the best in your class, that's not okay.

Go and ask all those children who want to study, and are willing to study, but their parents cannot afford to educate them. They would tell you how blessed you are. For everything your parents are doing for you, they have only one expectation from you. They want you to do well with your studies and in all other activities of your school life. That's the minimum you can do for them.

8

I am pursuing a course in Chartered Accountancy. I am unable to organise my schedule of studies. Please help me to organise myself.

If there is one aspect of life where there is no partiality it is with regards to 'Time'. From a king to a beggar, from a super success to a super failure, everybody has only 24 hours in a day. Time is the most important raw material for success. If I ask you to crush 24 rupees and throw it in the dustbin, you won't. Yet, so many 24 hours are dumped aimlessly. It is in knowing the value of time one understands the value of life. Time gets used up even if you do not use it. That's why time is considered the ultimate of all resources. Get the most out of your time and thus you will get the most out of your life.

In limited-overs cricket, if I have to score 434 in 50 overs, then I will play the game differently. If I have to score only 200, then I will play differently. So how I use my 50 overs, depends on what I want to achieve in 50 overs. Similarly, what you do with your time depends upon what you want to achieve with your life. Now that you are clear that you want to be a Chartered Accountant, it is so much easier to get your priorities right.

You can't aspire to be a world champion in chess without giving enough time to chess. You can't desire to be a world champion in chess, but also say, 'IPL is coming, then my cousin is visiting us from the US...' Right now your focus on becoming a Chartered Accountant should take precedence over everything else. The time to plan your future is now. Life is all about focus. When I know what to focus upon then I will know where to invest my time. And the timeless principle is, "That on which you invest time, grows."

It is not that you do not have the time, but time is getting spent in the wrong pockets and some re-organisation is required. For example, three hours is going into watching TV and one hour is going into studies. They have to be re-organised. I am not going to tell you don't watch TV. But give the three hours to studies and the one hour to TV.

You have the voice of M S Subbulakshmi but will you scale similar heights - that's the question. You may - you may not. She knew the importance of it and gave all her time to music - will you? That's the question. If you do, what's not possible?

You have the acumen of Viswanathan Anand but will you be a world champion - that's the question. You may - you may not. He knew the importance of it and gave all his time to chess - will you? That's the question. If you do, what's not possible?

Great people are great because they give enough and more of their time to what is important without waiting for it to become urgent. When the right quantum of time goes to the right activities, then you will get your life right.

The entire future is waiting for you. I will see you at the top. ●

9

How do I build self-belief?

You build your self-belief by getting the direction of your intelligence right. It is not your intelligence, but it is the direction of your intelligence that determines what you become in life.

A geography teacher couldn't tolerate the naughtiness of a group of students in her class. Pappu was the naughtiest of them all. She called out to him, "Hey Pappu! Come here and show me where America is in this world map?" Pappu confidently walked up to the world map and with effortless ease put his finger on America. The teacher felt silenced. She asked Pappu to return to his seat and continued with the class. She spoke, "Now tell me, who discovered America?" The class screamed back in one voice, "Pappu!"

Neither Pappu nor the class lacked intelligence. True, they were naughty, but naughtiness is only misdirected intelligence. With the direction of intelligence right, there is no limit to what naughty people can achieve in their life. Naughtiness when directed properly is called creativity and creativity is a great asset.

Let me explain creativity through another story...

There was a department store which was doing very well. Unfortunately, in the very adjacent building another department store was opened, and a board was placed outside that store, 'Everyday lowest prices'. On the other side too one more department store was opened and there too a board was placed, which read, 'Everyday highest quality'. With 'Everyday lowest prices' on one side and 'Everyday highest quality' on the other side what are the chances of the department store in the middle? That's where creativity comes in! The department store in the middle - simply placed a board outside his store that read, 'Main Entrance'.

It is not your intelligence but the direction of your intelligence that determines what you become in life. So, you got to believe that by just getting the direction of your intelligence right, you can become what you want to become in life.

Speaking about the direction of your intelligence, there are 'Right ways to feel like a Hero' and 'Wrong ways to feel like a Hero', and it is crucial that your intelligence is directed in the right ways.

Either way you can feel like a hero, but there is one huge difference. When you choose the right way to feel like a hero, you will feel like a hero and you will also create yourself in the process. When you choose the wrong way to feel like a hero, no doubt you will feel like a hero, but you will destroy yourself in the process.

Get the direction of your intelligence right and build a strong self-belief.

“

It is not your intelligence but
the direction of your intelligence
that determines
what you become in life.

mahātria

After completing my 12th,
I have taken civil engineering,
and that's what my heart
wanted. Everyone I have met
says that this isn't for girls.
Do you think I was right in not
listening to others?

I have repeatedly empowered the world by calling out, "Come... Let us go the other way." So, what do you think my answer will be? Path breakers are pathfinders. Even assuming it isn't for the girls, won't it be amazing if you could be a trailblazer? If you do not break with the traditional past, you cannot create a breakthrough in the future.

It is one thing to try and run ahead of the rest in a time-tested path. It needs courage to run completely in a different direction. And, be sure, life paves the way for a resolute soul. And be even more certain that one day the world will follow you in your new path. The heart has conquered greater frontiers than the mind of a person. Even the greatest of intellectuals achieved legendary possibilities only when they pursued the passions of their heart. To subordinate the passions of the heart and to live a life of mere mental exploration will amount to prostituting your soul, no matter what may be the material gains.

Your heart sought civil engineering and you have gone ahead... That's it! And, that's right for you. I am not ridiculing the opinions of others. I am only saying the opinion of others is right from where they see it, but not from where your heart sees. Hey, if I am in the driver's seat, I can only drive based on my reflexes and not by the opinions of all my fellow passengers. The clearance they see is right but that's from their seat, and that hardly matters. The only thing that matters is what I see from my driver's seat.

Civil engineering is a great opportunity to do something truly legendary. Do you know that the icon of every city and every nation is actually an architectural creation? The Taj Mahal or the Great Wall or the White House or the Eiffel Tower or the monuments that depict each of the cities... So, getting into architecture or in your case civil engineering... at least makes you step into a field of legendary possibilities... Now it all depends on how much you expect out of yourself. Do you want to be just another one in the crowd or the one above the crowd?

You have a chance to do something truly iconic. And in doing so, you can become an icon. Then, generations to come, they will never say, "A girl shouldn't do civil engineering." ●

“

Life paves the way
for a resolute soul.
And be even more certain
that one day the world will follow you
in your new path.

mahātria

I am studying in 12th standard. I know some of my friends are not on the right track. If I don't go with them, I will lose them. If I go with them, I will lose myself. I need help.

Adolescence is an age when you crave for identity. Anything, if it gives you identity, then you will do it. All that matters is that you have to be recognised. You have to be noticed. Right or wrong isn't the question. Will it gain attention is the question! All that matters during teen-years is that identity.

Just because some of the cows go in that direction, so will the rest. Just because one pig ran in one direction the rest too will follow. Just because they did it, you too will do it. That's herd mentality. Not thinking by yourself; not thinking for yourself; just blindly following the crowd. Peer acceptance - that's all matters. Your friends should accept you. You should be part of the gang. They should not laugh at you. You should not feel isolated. You should not feel left out. So, you end up doing whatever others do.

If a few of your classmates smoke, you too are tempted to take a puff. If they browse wrong websites, you feel you too must. If they cut classes, then you too want to join the bandwagon. If they nickname a teacher, you too join the crowd. Right or wrong is not the question. Will I be seen as a hero, is the question? Beware! This is why 90 out of 100 people during their adolescent years lose focus in their lives and end up being a mediocre - living a below average life.

Temptations of life during adolescent years are like thorns. Your life, during this phase, is like a piece of cloth. It is better to ensure it doesn't fall on the thorns at all. It is easier to never touch a cigarette than to struggle later to give up smoking. It is better to never get into a relationship of infatuation than to come out of the emotional trauma of a broken relationship. It is better not to fall than to struggle to rise from the fall. After all, once the cloth is fallen on the thorns, no matter how carefully you take it out - the cloth would still get damaged.

Develop the right circle of friends. Friends at this stage have the power to make you or break you. Shun the company of anyone who gives you the slightest of hints to mislead you in life. It is better to walk alone and be right, than to be part of a crowd and be wrong. One or two quality friends are more than enough.

To get your life right, get your teenage years right and to get your teenage years right, get your friends right. I know you will immediately ask me, how will I know who are the right friends? Anything you will have to hide from your parents, whatever may be your reasons, the very thought that you want to hide it from your parents - then you know it is wrong. Find the right friends. And more importantly, be the right friend. ●

You have to be noticed.
Right or wrong
isn't the question.
Will it gain attention
is the question!
All that matters
during teen-years
is that identity.

mahātria

12

A wrong is a wrong,
no matter who does it,
even if it is your parents.
We are also told, irrespective
of anything and everything,
we must be grateful to
our parents. Please clarify.

If consistency and objectivity has to be practiced in life then the focus should be, "What is right or wrong," and never, "Who is right or wrong". We should be issue-based and not person-based. It is in that context that right is right and wrong is wrong - no matter who is involved in it.

However, also understand, you cannot remove the nose because you have a running nose. You cannot remove the head for headache. Whether it is parents or others, right and wrong is about the 'act' and not the person. Mahatma Gandhi rightly put it when he said, "Hate the sin. Love the sinner."

In matters of right and wrong, it is only righteous to be objective even with parents. Yet, what your parents 'do or do not do' should never alter your gratitude for them. After all, all that you 'did and did not' didn't alter their love for you in grooming you.

13

*I am an average student.
I always score average marks.
I want to improve my academic performance. Can you give me useful tips to follow?*

Here are a few ways in which you can make studies more interesting, enjoyable, fun, and most importantly something that really works.

Identify your learning style:

Each individual has their own unique way of learning, but in general, there are three common types of learning styles: Visual, Auditory, and Kinaesthetic. Every person has one predominant learning mode. If a student can identify their predominant style, they can enhance the process of learning in a more effective way.

Visual students learn best from what they see. You know you are visual, when your basic languaging is, "The moment I saw the formula. Do you see the point? Look, I am trying to tell you..." If you are visual, your best learning methodology will be to see your books, look into your notes, watch the board attentively, study silently and avoid group studies.

Auditory students learn best from what they hear. You know you are auditory, when your basic languaging is, "The day I heard the formula. Are you listening to my point? Hey, listen..." If you are auditory, your best learning methodology will be to read aloud, listen to your teachers and take up group studies.

Kinaesthetic students learn best from what they feel. You know you are kinaesthetic, when your basic languaging is, "I feel this formula is easy. Are you with me? If you can't feel what I am talking about, there is no point..." If you are kinaesthetic, your best learning methodology will be though laborious, but can't help it, you have to write and practice; study without distractions and avoid group studies.

Remember, no one learning style is better than another. Each has its own advantages and drawbacks, depending on what you're trying to learn. Adapt to your learning style and you will make learning easier and more enjoyable. Of course, you should know that those who make it to the top bracket in academics practice all the three learning methodologies - they read it, they say it and also they write and practice it. That's why it makes so much of a difference to them because they don't leave any learning methodology to chance.

Plan 50-minute hour:

The average attention span of most human beings is only 45 to 50 minutes. The human mind needs distraction to stay attracted. So, always study for a maximum period of 50 minutes and then gift yourself a 10-minute distraction. Please ensure it is not the other way around, that you stay distracted for 50 minutes and for a change study for 10 minutes.

Maintain a key-point notebook:

Maintain a notebook in which you write down all the key points as you keep studying, and it will help you immensely before your exams. It will be enough if you can just revise the key points from this notebook.

Identify your peak hours:

Every individual has different peak hours. For some, night studies suit them the best, for others it is early morning, and for quite a few it is daytime preparation. Peak hours vary from person to person. Identify your peak hours and commit that time to your studies. There is no point in watching Virat Kohli bat during your peak hours. Virat Kohli should bat during his peak hours. You must study during your peak hours. Your lazy hours can go in watching TV.

Choose a space for study:

You pray in the *pooja* room, take a bath in the bathroom and do experiments in a laboratory. Similarly, there has to be a dedicated space for studies. Let it just be a corner in the house, maybe the balcony, could be the terrace - but there has to be a dedicated space for studies.

Practice a ritual before studying:

Always practice some ritual before you begin your studies. It could be offering a prayer, it could be chanting, it could be something you always write before you begin, but develop a ritual before you begin your studies. This ritual will send a message to your intelligence that you're going to start studying and it must to concentrate. It really helps.

I know education is such a tough task in the life of a student. But, it is worth it. It will make all the difference to your life. If you spend a few sleepless nights now, you will sleep well for the rest of your life. Don't sleep too much now and be sleepless for the rest of your life. If you are going to be tough on yourself, life will be infinitely easy on you. If you are easy on yourself, life will be very tough on you.

Make your parents proud. Make your teachers proud. And be proud of yourself. ●

Remember, no one learning style
is better than another.
Each has its own advantages
and drawbacks, depending on
what you're trying to learn.
Adapt to your learning style
and you will make learning easier
and more enjoyable.

mahātria

14

*There are good and bad habits.
I have my share of bad habits.
Despite my knowledge, the lure
is so overwhelming that most
of the time I am unable to resist.
Is there a way out?*

Habits, good or bad, disturb one's flow and happiness. Hence they are wrong. Habits are mental phonograph records. Repeated indulgence in anything creates a mental blueprint. Whenever one puts the needle of attention on the grooves formed in the mind, it plays back the blueprint. Repetition causes the grooves to deepen and after a while, the record plays automatically, over and over again. The mental make-up, the patterns called habit become hard set, making it difficult to change. Thus we become slaves to our habits and lose our freedom, self-discipline and control. Our habits make us lead a robot-like existence.

Ivan Pavlov used to ring a metronome at the same time he fed his dogs. After a while, the dogs that earlier salivated only on seeing their food, began to salivate when the metronome sounded, even if no food was present. Imagine a person suffering like Pavlov's dogs? But that's what habits are - ring the bell and they will salivate.

If you do not get what you want when you want it, and it disturbs you, it has gained mastery over you. What has gained mastery over you has gained mastery over your peace. The more the number of external masters you have, the less peaceful you are.

If the newspaper is delayed, it disturbs your peace. If the coffee is not to your specification, it disturbs your peace. If you can't go to the temple when you want to, it disturbs your peace. Even going to places of worship has become a conditioned mechanical response - a habit. If going or not going to the temple disturbs your peace, then even your relationship with the force above has become habitual. That which does not give you peace and that which disturbs your peace, can never be classified as spirituality.

The proof of right living is in the peace that you experience. Habits disturb your peace and hence all habits are wrong. You can overcome habits only through 'Willpower', and 'Willpower' is developed through 'Won't Power'. The next time you don't get something when you want it, and it disturbs you, understand it has gained mastery over you. Practice 'Won't Power'. For one full week abstain from that which disturbed you. If necessary get back to it after a week. But if not getting it when you want it continues to disturb you, practice 'Won't Power' again for another week... till you either gain complete mastery over it or no more need it, forever. Take it one week at a time and achieve a triumph of a lifetime.

Everything that comes into our life should either stay with us to become our strength, or it should leave us to make us free. It should never stay with us and become our weakness. ●

You can overcome habits only through 'Willpower', and 'Willpower' is developed through 'Won't Power'.

mahātria

15

My long time aim is to learn a new language. To learn a new language should we learn to read and write or just learn to read?

Depends on what you want to do with the new language. If it is for reading and writing then you must practice reading and writing. However, if you want to communicate in that language then the most crucial factor is an environment with that language.

Haven't we seen people who have academically mastered a language but because they do not have the environment to converse in that language they can never become communicators in that language. On the contrary, a South Indian with absolutely no exposure to Hindi gets employed in Delhi for two years and develops fluency in conversational Hindi. We have also seen so many graduates who settle into domestic life, lack an environment to speak in English, hence few years later struggle to communicate fluently in English.

So, for any spoken language to be developed, an environment with that language is mandatory. That's why learning a new language in a group is always more beneficial than solo-learning. ●

My parents are okay with sending me abroad for my higher studies but my grandparents are not convinced about this. How do I convince them? It is important for me that they are happy with this decision.

A man is nothing more than his mind; a mind is nothing more than patterns of thoughts. We all have certain patterns of thoughts. For example 'if you send a girl abroad we don't know what she will do' is a pattern of thought that has been passed on for many generations now.

The advantage with thoughts is, if we keep on cueing in new thoughts onto existing thought patterns, one day these new thoughts will become more dominant than old patterns. These new thoughts will become our current thought patterns.

To cue in new thoughts, to erase the old patterns and replace it with new patterns, we need to communicate long enough.

This is how Mahatma Gandhi was able to achieve independence for India. Britons did not leave India, the moment Mahatma Gandhi said 'Quit India'; they put him in jail and he continued to say the same thing. On his release Gandhiji realised that he alone saying 'Quit India' to Britons is not creating the change; so he communicated to his people and convinced them also to say it. He gained the support of his fellow men and together they repeatedly said, 'Quit India' in every possible way – through their voice and actions. All of them were jailed and when they were released more people joined Gandhiji – it became a movement. History shows that eventually Britons quit India.

Gandhi taught us something - if you can communicate long enough even the mighty British Empire's mind can be changed. Are you willing to communicate long enough?

Getting irritated, getting angry, being disrespectful is not going to help. Communicate long enough; there is no mind that cannot be changed if you are willing to communicate long enough patiently.

In your case, you have the support of your parents. Communicate with your grandparents long enough about your focus on the future, your potential and capability, and most importantly, tell them that you will be morally right and will not defame the family. That is their fear now.

Somebody in their circle might have gone astray after going abroad and that is the thought pattern they have right now. Change their thought pattern by communicating long enough by citing examples of students who have gone abroad and become achievers while continuing to be morally right. Become one such role model who will be quoted in your family for generations to come. ●